A MURDER OF CROWS

New & Selected Poems

ALSO BY RICHARD STEVENSON

Driving Offensively
(Sono Nis Press, 1985)

Suiting Up
(Third Eye Publications, 1985)

Horizontal Hotel: A Nigerian Odyssey
(TSAR Publications, 1989)

Whatever It Is Plants Dream...
(Goose Lane Editions, 1990)

Learning To Breathe
(Cacanadadada Press, 1992)

From The Mouths of Angels
(Ekstasis Editions, 1993)

Flying Coffins
(Ekstasis Editions, 1994)

Why Were All The Werewolves Men?
(Thistledown Press,1994)

Wiser Pills
(HMS Books-on-Disk, 1995)

A MURDER OF CROWS

New & Selected Poems

Richard Stevenson

BLACK MOSS PRESS

1998

Published by Black Moss Press, 2450 Byng Road, Windsor, Ontario N8W 3E8. Black Moss Press books are distributed by Firefly Books, 3680 Victoria Park Ave., Willowdale, Ontario, M2H 3K1. All orders should be directed there.

Black Moss Press would like to acknowledge the support of the Department of Canadian Heritage.

We would also like to acknowledge the support of the Canada Council for the Arts for our publishing program.

CANADIAN CATALOGUING IN PUBLICATION DATA

Stevenson, Richard, 1952-
    A murder of crows

Poems.
ISBN 0-88753-317-5

    I. Title.

PS8587.T479M88 1998   C811'.54   C98-900977-7
PR9199.3.S84M88 1998

The bulk of the poems in this selection have been published previously or previously accepted for publication in the following chapbooks and full-length collections:

Hierarchy At the Feeder (dollarpoems editions, 1984), **Suiting Up** (Third Eye Publishing, 1985), **Driving Offensively** (Sono Nis Press, 1985), **Twelve Houseplants** (dollarpoem editions, 1985), **Horizontal Hotel: A Nigerian Odyssey** (TSAR Publications, 1989), **Whatever It Is Plants Dream...** (Goose Lane Editions, 1990), **Learning To Breathe** (Ronsdale (then Cacanadadada) Press, 1992), **From The Mouths Of Angels** (Ekstasis Editions, 1993), **Flying Coffins** (Ekstasis Editions, 1994), **Wiser Pills** (HMS Books-on-Disk, 1995), **A Dog Named Normal** (Egorag Editions) and **Body Sculpture** (Reference West, forthcoming).

My thanks to the editors and publishers concerned for their support and encouragement. Thanks also to the editors of all the literary/arts magazines, newsletters, journals, and anthologies who first accepted these poems, or earlier versions of them for publication. The new poems first appeared in *Whetstone* and *Revelek*.

Thanks also to my parents, Robert James and Marguerite Stevenson, for their unstinting support, and to my many friends and colleagues – in Canada, The United States, England, Australia, Nigeria, Sierra Leone, and wherever else they may have wandered since we broke bread or cola nuts – for comments, criticism, friendship, bookswaps, readings, and all the gentle prodding that have taken me this far.

Finally, my most heartfelt thanks to my wife, Gepke, without whose patience, editorial input, and superhuman endurance the past twenty years' gleanings would never have seen light of day.

This book is for Gepke, Marika, Adrian, and Christian: four legs of a family table that has seen much bounty and beneficence.

Cover designed by John Doherty.

TABLE OF CONTENTS

I. SUITING UP (1985)

The Elizabethans Called It " Little Death"	9
The Brigadier	10
Two Hundred Ton of Potatoes	14
Murder In The Kitchen	16
Victim Of The Oldest Fish	17
The Coats	18
He Sees Himself In The Dishes	19

II. DRIVING OFFENSIVELY (1985)

Sunday Sermon, Wulari Ward	23
Mohammed and Gretel	24
Hunting Pythons	25
Shake Hands and Your Genitals Will Disappear	26
Routing Out Thieves	28
Mr. Crapper I Presume?	30

III. HORIZONTAL HOTEL (1989)

Why Does It Cry So?	33
Rinse Cycle	34
Traffic Fatalities	35
Building Flaws	36
The Child's Head	37
The Worm In The Meat Is Also Meat	38

IV. WHATEVER IT IS PLANTS DREAM ... (1990)

Bird of Paradise	41
Prayer Plant	42
Spider Plant	43
Boston Fern	44
Moses-in-the-Cradle (Oyster Plant)	45

V. LEARNING TO BREATHE (1992)

Another Hansel And Gretel Story	49
Henry, In Mid-Leap	56
Condom Tales	57
Poem After a Photograph in MOTHER JONES	60
Beijing Massacre	61
New Black Shoes	62
Shhh, They're Sleeping	63
Telefomin Trousers	64

VI. From the Mouths of Angels (1993)

Improvisation For Two Hummingbirds   69
Lovebird   71
Amadeus Macaw   73
From The Mouths of Angels   74
The Tallest Totem   75
Quick's Bottom   76

VII. Flying Coffins (1994)

The World According To Reuter   79
Zavin, On The Night Shift   80
Upside-down Tree   82

VIII. Wiser Pills (1995)

Dick and Jane Have Sex   85
Frank's Aquarium   87
Howard's Teeth   91
Making An Angel for Bob   92
Big Al's Trick   94
Not by My Chinny Chin Chin   95
Vasectomy   97

IX. New Poems

The Canadian Guide To Death and Dying   100
The Embolism   105
Talking Back To Zoloft   107
Boy in a Red Shirt on a Trampoline   111

I

SUITING UP

-1985-

The Elizabethans Called It " Little Death "

This morning while we were
making love in our bed,
a bird flew headlong
into the window pane.

A perfect three-point landing
foiled. Your breasts warm as
sparrows cupped in my hands
as you got up to pull the drapes.

I watched my reflection
slide from your eyes,
beneath their sills
as you intoned, " poor bird, "

thought of the final still photo
that might be focused
on the retina of its eyes,
where we might be
before they closed.

A simple mistake –
not being able to tell
the forest for the trees,

and it scares me to think
I always look into your eyes
when I say I love you
in times like these.

the words forever frozen
in parentheses
like that bird,
that tree.

The Brigadier

1.

Once Brigadier in His Majesty's service,
he showed me chests inlaid with ivory
bought for a song on the Gold Coast,
ships he'd made in bottles,
rigging, ropes, not a rope or sail
out of place. Spry cordage of his face
animate, coiled about his eyes. Not lies
or half-truths, everything done in miniature.
He would taunt me to tell him
how anyone could make anything
to such exacting standards and
get them through the neck of a bottle.
I would propose cutting the bottle in half,
or cutting the bottom off, pulling
the rigging upright with a string.
Later, when he drank upwards of a bottle
of rye a day, he wrote stories:
adventures: heroic themes hobbled to
weak-kneed plots, foreign syntax
stumbling through the misspelled words,
staggering down the page.
He would ask me where to send them
to be published,
in his more lucid moments, what
needed to be done to effect repairs,
his eyes floating over a sea of faces,
seeking retribution, a new land.

2.

Every morning the same ritual: hacking up the phlegm,
an old handkerchief stuffed in at the hole,
the body's engine choked, primed,
he dressed the wound. Memories:
old rags around the pipes;
consciousness built up like a head of steam.

Legs over the side of the bed,
stretching, rubbing eyes, neck,
thoughts palpable, soft –
retractible as a snail,
whisked back into the bottle.

Pushing the proud prow into
deeper waters.

3.

For his wife
only the promise,
the aroma and sanction
of morning coffee with
the neighbours.

her days met out
as from an abacus:
raindrops on a line.
Wisps of cloud snapped
clean as laundry in her mind.

Motes of light gathered
a collusion of particles,
molecules dancing before
her pinprick eyes.
Thoughts settled like dust
onto the furniture.

4.

Memory a wilderness of his making:
he liked to fish
places where other animals
came to slake their thirst;
water striders would twitch
like a nervous tic
above a stranger's eye,
his reflection blurting,
moving out in concentric circles
into all recesses of his mind.

Downstream, a huge bear pawing
fish out of the water:
a time before he had his camera
or a gun. Eyes sighting
the beast in very mirror...

In a dream
space clean and white
lay before him like a tablecloth.
The sun began to climb
like a fly upon the wall.

The sentences grew shorter:
a shower of pebbles
shot from a sling.

Birds came to the treetop
of his nerves. Sometimes
he would change from third
to first person in
the middle of a paragraph

or just stare outside his window,
watching the smoke rise
from the neighbour's chimney:

plumed feather of
the peacock
strutting among their days.

5.

Always pissed they said;
finally, pissed out:
his eyes like dying coals
smouldering way back in his brain.

His system backed up
like a sewer drain.
He was drunk for days
without a drop.

Wife found him one night
sitting upright in a chair,
paralyzed, brain transfixed
like a huge butterfly
under the weight of his eyes.
He died two days later in hospital.

Uremia they said.
All the stories, clothes, personal effects
tamed in a drawer, released;
the funeral was a simple one.

All the old hands on deck
played him out until the end.
Standing in the penumbra of his shadow,
they spoke of him fondly,
with more than just
a modicum of respect.

As though to pat him on the shoulders,
they bore him up like epaulettes.
Carefully, they consigned him to the ground,
a ship in his own bottle.
" Once Brigadier in His Majesty's Service ... "
With him went the rubric,
a thousand year old egg.

Two Hundred Ton of Potatoes

in memoriam Peter Polet

"It has been a really
wet fall and winter.
Two hundred ton of potatoes
had to be left in the ground,"
your father writes:

and I imagine him
hunched over the immaculate
gingham of the table cloth,
scratching, stubbing out each word
like the cigarettes he smokes half way.

Between coughs he lays out the sentences
end to end like irrigation pipes,
butts them together to make
a conduit that will take
three weeks to get here, possibly four.

One by one the periods settle:
dark birds hopping amongst the cuttings
and refuse at the far side of the field.
Cigarettes smoulder in the ashtray
like stumps bulldozed to make vacant lots.

There was a time he would lean
on his words as on a shovel;
the gumboot ball of his foot
came down with his full weight,
the weight of the sun:

they bit deep into the earth
to wrest the past from the suck
and drag of the mud.
he held the clotted gems; one by one,
washed them under the cold
taps of reason and hope;

a time he would turn the green skins
over and over in the palm of his hand,
with tuberous fingers to show us
the toxin that spoiled
the flesh of each lobe.

Now the words have thinner skins
than they once did; irrevocable,
are buried deep. They too
must be left in the ground
to proliferate their errant cells.
Now we listen to what the potatoes would tell

had they mouths as well as eyes
that could send up shoots that didn't lie.

Maiduguri, Nigeria 4/82

Murder In The Kitchen

Was it something in the noise
the streetlights made,
louder than the hum
of the frigidaire?
Was it something in the air?
A full moon. That sleeve of darkness
on which it battened like a moth?
A ten watt bulb,
a door swung open in the night ...
Was it fright that frightened
the fear away;
a pseudopod of blue
leaking from the T.V. screen?
Something in the shadows unseen,
domestic shrubs cropped like poodles
that rubbed against each door?
A bag of groceries leaning at the stoop/
another threshold/ a series of scenes
taken in dull transfusion
out of walls:
synopsis of circumstance:
a walk to the grocery store;
the facts, nothing but the facts,
nothing more. The blood red
of sunset on the countertop
draining away from the eye
like blood from a steak:
intent: thoughts set out as daily bread?
Before sleep, came the dream:
we had furniture that talked,
would formulate whole sentences
about the placement of a shoe
or coat or person leaving;
the front door was a mouth
that never quit.
Then we grew hungry,
waiting for Our Master's Voice.
Was this what it was all along:
a needle dropping into song,
silence standing behind
the arras of our words,
satisfaction tracking intractable desire?

Victim Of The Oldest Fish

Dyspeptic, overweight, middle-aged,
surfeit with politics, religion,
morning coffee, two eggs,
toast and marmalade;
he belches, turns the page;
shifts the bolus of words
to the other side of his mouth perhaps,
eyes pouring over the flotsam and jetsam
beached up with the morning tide.

Sees two words bitten off,
bleeding from their stumps,
story trailing like entrails
in a column
down the second page:

"Shark, Mom!" —
Another twelve year old kid
barely able to bite off
a syllable or two
before it happened.

Language caught
in a feeding frenzy
of its own blood moil
gobbles him up,
spits him out.

Sunlight spreading its stain
between his hands,
he looks at his watch,
picks up his lunch bucket and coat,
hesitates before
filing away this anecdote.

Car already idling:
a cetacean with large dorsals,
sculling the air
to remain in one position,
barbel quivering
to find a curb somewhere;
his life swallows him like Jonah's whale.

His teeth don't bite,
they swim in a glass.

The Coats

Piled high as the corpses at Dachau or Belsen,
arms akimbo, nightmarishly joined;
or clapping each other on the shoulders,
sharing the strange brotherhood of survival,
beckoning like war amps
from the back of the closet;
space surrounds them,
brings them into stark relief:
a sculpture neat as Praxiteles' hair.

No scarecrows these –
hardy as the lumpen proletariat –
only coats. Their shadows
writhe on the wall
as on the head of some Medusa.
Guilt turned irrevocably to stone.

And yet, for a minute or two,
a kind of ceremonial silence attends them;
their names retract
as suddenly as their owners
leaving the room;
they seem somehow alive,
bloom like a colonial tubeworm
in our absence.
They feather the slow eddies of air,
gathering evidence, food;
hold us to the shape we've
made of them.

He Sees Himself In The Dishes

Tonight they are in fine form.
Dap, dap, dap, his tongue
a one-inch finishing brush
applies the satin latex to
the delicately fluted molding
around the window of her ear.

Slowly he unrolls the sheath –
gossamer-thin, smooth as silk,
stretches it, smoothes it down:
a strip of American rose
wallpaper perfectly aligned,
carefully applied, design sides
for once matching up perfectly.

The whole thing leaves no bubble
between the earth and sky.
"I love you," he says. "I love you too,"
she replies – and they mean it;
it is as if someone up there
on the ladder really were
going to paint a cow, and
the moon were a fresh can
of one-coat, didn't need a primer
of blue sky to fill up the pores.

The cow stayed at the end of
that shaft of light a long time,
its udder a pair of rubber gloves,
the pools of its eyes tepid
as tap water; and from the
rich suds of those Bo-Peep clouds,
a white plate emerged in which
the face of a man was clearly discernible,
the stars' cutlery sparkled, really shone.

II
DRIVING OFFENSIVELY
-1985-

(Nigeria 1980 - 1982)

Sunday Sermon, Wulari Ward

Spitting, lashing out, recoiling,
he fights for the Word:
a black mongoose
caught in the languorous coils
of electric cords and couplings.

And yet there is something
of the snake in him too.
Leaflets hang back legs from
the body of his book,
his fist jerks at each
slippery segment of truth.

He thumps a fifty gallon drum –
empty pulpit of an oil-rich state –
with the flat of his other hand,
and the wide-eyed children of Wulari
rock back and forth on their heels.

Their bodies move
enmass, in waves
to catch the rhythm,
if not the drift, and take
the hard bolus of his words.

There was a time they
would have laughed
and swallowed this white
juju all in good fun.
Now they stand in fear and tremble.

They are awed by the white lily
of a black man's megaphone.
Stare, intent, as it flares
briefly in this sand
then withers and dies in silence.

Then, thirsty for something other
than its electric, intoxicating perfume,
they eye my Coke, stare at me.
Being white, visible as that megaphone,
hemmed in by the dark rosary of their eyes,
I swallow once. Pass the bottle on.

Mohammed and Gretel

In the first frame
the bear and boy
come face-to-face:

Disney cherubs
with little O mouths
and sweet button eyes,

do their best
to look dismayed,
float like seraphim
from the page.

In the next frame
the big brown bear
has a big brown belly:

there is neither
hide nor hair
of the little white boy.

You ask the class
what has happened,
tell them to finish
the little toy fable.

Charity, Hauwa, Fanta,
all the form three's
are firmly convinced:

the bear is pregnant, madam;
the boy he go
for his work.

Hunting Pythons

Are there a lot of snakes around here?
How do you catch them when they're
so big and dangerous, I ask,
slowly sliding my wallet out.

Make you wait some times. No 'fraid.
Dey no de bite wid you too much.
Make dem swallow comme ca, finish.
Dem eyes no be good too much –
I tink you sabe, ba?
Make you hide for grass.
You commot you arm comme ca,
dem go smell 'um chop. Den dey come.
No 'fraid, na grease. You arm no go stay
in 'im belly. You hol' 'im 'andle
tight too much. 'im blade be rest fo' arm.
'e be no problem. You dey cut am for inside
comme quick quick for outside. 'e go die.
You go hi 'im head, finish –
das all. Dem no go squeeze you kuma.
You gettam for friend? 'e not be too much.
Mastah? Naira fifty last – for you, customer.
Make you bring money, mastah – come!
Naira fifty for de two – 'e no be too much.
You go hang dem for wall. 'e be nice, not so?

His and hers skins
on the wall of the rec room, I think;
my son's eyes'd light up for sure –
then thought throws me another loop:
he has to make a living; this is a big bite –
no telling when the next meal'd be.
I.D. papers and bills
stick out of my wallet like feet.

Shake Hands and Your Genitals Will Disappear

There is trouble on the playing field:
you have words spread out
like a line of fearful citizens
looking for some kind of clue.

The look that comes over the children's faces
tells you it is going to rain soon,
and so you would hurry home, but you can't
get away from that either.

There is a man sitting in your office
and those are real sticks, real stones
the children are reaching for. The man
is evil and the children are coming

like a shadow, a cloud or airplane
passing slowly overhead; it's not
cats and dogs that will fall, but blows,
for one among them has shaken hands –

two, three: all are convinced
the man has made their genitals
grow smaller, if not disappear.
They want a girl just to make sure.

Bring am. Make them drop their drawers.
Show them how much smaller yours is
if you have to. It has come to that.
Tell them the world hangs like a clapper

between their knees. Tell them you should be
so lucky to be hung the way they are.
Laugh the laugh that sends syllables
scurrying into every nook and cranny of truth.

The words you give them as tools
lay still as blood on the page,
yet their fingers will fidget and twitch,
yet they will reach for their sticks.

You split their skulls wide to reveal brains
unfolding like roses. Name all the parts.
Yet they would eat the truth raw,
stare at you with the eyes of a mantis.

You promise them higher pay,
education, your words tumescent with truth,
and still, when their pants come down,
meaning shrinks as pupils from light.

They see themselves wizened,
their manhood, their future
shrunk to the size
of two black-eyed peas.

Routing Out Thieves

In Onitsha, the story goes,
the market mamas, fed up
with the rash of crime,
the loss of property and lives,
took matters in their hands.

Swarmed the warehouse cache
of stolen T.V.s. cloth, and stereos
before cockcrow. Routed out
the thieves who, red-eyed,
dazed, had only time to see

the hubbub of pointed sticks,
blades and arrows trained
on them. To catch the gist
of tires hooping them like pegs,
splash of petrol, spurt of match.

Cursed, screamed, prayed to
whatever gods were breaking
the brittle calabash of blood and bone,
blistered and boiled skin
away from slack bowels, the ureic hiss.

Time then to burn with even flame
in the pilot lights of victims' eyes,
eyes that had seen Biafra, the genocide
of Ibo tribesmen by the Hausa here
where petro dollars build new roads.

Now rumour travels faster than
the "flying coffins" between towns.
"Ladies delegations" go
to Maiduguri, Jos, Kaduna, Kano
where fresh outbreaks of theft are spoken of.

Fear fans a brush fire
in the open Sahel, goes underground to smoulder
in the trash heap of every citizen's heart
where he hears of the bright necklace of blood
that girdles a sleeping miguardi's neck.

The batures' eyes,
full of dust and "leper bits,"
blink, careen like pollen-laden
bumblebees about the open pistils
of green bottles on the tabletops,

fall into the open corolla
of luxuriant, exotic petals,
the circle of a few familiar faces
in the photographs they take
and never get out of themselves.

Mr. Crapper I Presume?

Before Mshelia sits the toilet:
strange, exotic as a diagram
in his biology textbook –
the shell-like cochlea
of his inner ear, he thinks.

How does one approach it?
He loosens his belt,
steps out of his milieu
as easily as he steps
out of his trousers.

Faces it squarely,
grasps both sides
of the cistern firmly,
then steps aboard.
So far so good.

Remains only the skill
required to take aim,
make the hoop
before the lug bolts loosen
and down comes Mshelia
cistern, science, and all.

Now the white man
and all egg-headed
inventors' contraptions
can go to hell. Mshelia
will not be put together
their way again.

III

HORIZONTAL HOTEL

-1989-

(Nigeria 1980 - 1982)

Why Does It Cry So?

Why does it cry so? Mohammed asks,
our electric iron sputtering, spewing
water in his hand. Why does ours cry
when his doesn't? I think: electricity,
heating coil, boiling water, steam.

How marvellous that he should be
so ignorant of this thing we take for granted;
how exciting to be able to see
God's mysterious ways working
the creases into my pants.

How sad that Mohammed
should feel the compunction to be
so goddamned polite in asking us
if he could use ours to iron his.
We feel embarrassed and humbled too

that ours should have such a forked tail
and depend on such transfusions
as the god of electricity will allow.
How far the cord has really stretched
that we should find our shirts
floating like kites with so many keys attached.

Rinse Cycle

A picture of maternity
such as Grandma Moses
might have painted it:

Knitpurl, knitpurl, pause:
madam puts down her knitting,
bends to her steward an ear –

almost like the RCA Victor
pooch before the Victrola
listening for her Master's voice.

Scrub, scrub, swish – yes,
it's the laundry all right,
but the intermittent flush?

She gets up to check,
and sure enough: Sale's
discovered a better way

than the grape-squashing,
knees-up-Mother-Brown
method in the tub.

Almost listening itself,
the porcelain ear of the toilet
receives her episcopal shirts.

Traffic Fatalities

Where we come from
the roads are paved;
bodies break like eggs
onto a surface clean
as a Teflon frying pan.

Children stare out back
windows of their daddies' cars,
watch landmarks shrink away
like the blue turn-off dots
on their T.V. screens.

The moon we remember
ran like a car through the trees,
or stood like a nurse in uniform
above the spinning wheels.
We counted foreign license plates.

Here the children grow up fast,
if they grow up at all.
Call for passengers
on a bus that goes to market.
We count bones. The twentieth century
a matter of fossil record:

forty-four wrecks between Bauchi and Jos,
sinking like mastodons into the sand.
Kanuri and Fulani villagers
step across time, certain that
animals with such big eyes will see.

Building Flaws

The new classroom wing
of the State Polytechnic
is finally finished.

Rebar and cinder block
held together with mortar
from head-carried hods,

propped up every few feet
with hand-hewn logs
and wadded handshakes.

Three floors, eighty blocks
for every forty budgeted
per bag of cement –

a child's recipe, the building
inspector will later maintain,
awaiting further ingredients;

a three-layer cake
in need of a little more
icing, a little leavening perhaps.

Perhaps a few more students,
a few more chocolate jimmies
sprinkled under mortar and dust.

The Child's Head

The child's head has been shaved,
looks like the pocked surface of another planet,
where men might leap a hundred feet
in almost zero gravity.
Flies, seen from a distance as spots,
might be a herd of lunar ruminants
stopping at the neighbourhood waterhole.

But there are no Bambies
drinking the cool waters of their reflections here,
nor will the language of this place scab over.
The fly that drinks from the child's eye
drinks freely. The child stares
through his own telescope
at the moon of my white skin.
Doesn't raise a finger, doesn't blink.

The Worm In The Meat Is Also Meat

Oga, make you listen now.
Na cola nut e split two ways:
Na dis way, na dat. E na be so?
Make you chop, make I chop.
I tink you sabe, ba?

You go give me small small cola,
I go do disting for you, finish;
you no go give me small small cola,
for how I go chop? I no go do disting for you.
You go make big palaver, I no go talk wid you.

Oga, I tink you be teacher, isn't it?
You be big man. You go havam steward,
you go havam misguardi; disting, dat.
You go for house wetin be de air condition,
you havam big motor, you go get money plenty.

Dis our Nigeria, dis no be your country, ba?
Dis country e give you senior staff house,
e give you water, e give you light ...
So how now? For why you make wahala here?
I no vex wid you. For why you vex wid me now?

Kai! You be stubborn man! You no havam ears?
You go pay me now, na you go pay dem plenty.
Is simple. E na be too much now! Kai!
You sabe book, e be big problem for you na
sabe "make I chop"? No holler am so-tay!

You tink I be idiot? You be idiot!
Na dis be one-plus-one now? Haba!
You tink I no go for school, isn't it?
You tink I no sabe dis your western
equality palaver, dis dem-o-cra-see ting.

I go for school! Den my fader e no chop proper.
I go for army for so. I make small small chop
for feed my family. I work am, I work am:
I no come rich for so. Dis cola make me bellyful.
Dis cola make me big man now, e na be so?

So no holler am wid me; I no go hear am.
Make you come back tomorrow, dis tomorrow e never come.
You go waka waka wi dis your paper, e never come.
I no go sign am, dem no go sign am.
Is simple. Na worm in dis meat, e na be meat?

38

IV

WHATEVER IT IS PLANTS DREAM ...

-1990-

Bird of Paradise
(Strelitzia reginae)

All the How To Grow
Healthy House Plant books
say the shape of its flowers
gave this one its name.

And it is true: one sees plumage
and spiky flame-like crest
of a noble, long-legged bird
that cocks its head quizzically,

listens patiently for that
snake-in-the-grass
of anthropomorphic male metaphor.
Some rare combination of stork

and secretary bird keeping tabs
on that first foundling word
that wormed its way through
Adam's apple, say. This one's

bullish on botany: rends
genus from differentia
and swallows the works
before we can say Darwin

or Genesis. Or ontogeny
recapitulates phylogeny.
The whole holus bolus
of language gets caught

like a half-swallowed snake
half-way down its straining
green throat. Other buds
waver like ungainly nestlings.

And why rot in paradise?
The moon fixed like a grub
to the thorn of an acacia tree.
Sun sharpening its cold cutlery

for the rich feast of binomials.
The plants were here first,
yet Adam, by dint of his intelligence,
must reach for and name.

Prayer Plant
(*maranta leuconeura*)

Each leaf's a trilobite,
a fossil record laid down
on the raised white
silt of incandescent light.
Today a laying on of hands,
tomorrow a peaked roof of prayer.

Its secret the curled leaf
raising an admonishing
finger to invisible lips.

These new leaves cajole
and unroll an ancient
scroll of palmate runes.

Try to catch them praying;
their numbers grow laterally,
stems grow droopish,
cascade over our pots.

Each leaf is its own millstone.
They ingratiate themselves before
the arras of what we
imagine a window to be.

Don't expect applause
from the one-hand clapping.

Spider Plant
(Chlorophytum comosum)

Take the cuttings, dunk the wounds
in a fine dust of rooting hormone:
pot their sibilant fountains of green:
well-placed incendiary bombs,
aimed at the softly-lit sill.
Their opulence spills, tumbles
like smoke into office windows and homes.

Growth a scattering, unheard shriek
in the bomb bay of genetic design:
they send out streamers, green runners,
plumes that explode on impact with air;
fill our cats-cradle, macramed space
with sibling paratroopers that hang
like spiders from phylogeny's thread.

Such an insect stillness in the compound
eye of these highrise windows at dawn.
A breeze riffles the torn chute of sky's
bismuthal hue. Theirs the kingdom this hour.
They dangle, wait for a green thought
to come like a butler, respond to
the frayed rope of ontogeny's call.

Boston Fern
(Nephrolepis exaltata)

This one's idea of opulence
is an ostrich-plumed hat
from a forgotten century.

Riding the pot with its tendrils
hanging like some fiery senorita's
lacquered kiss curls and wisps,

it supplants the air with
a thought as luxurious
and unreal as Juanita Banana's

wax fruit hat, a tacky
Fruitloops box cornucopia
presaging nattering toucans.

It outstrips the others' growth
to the point where its demands
for better housing have to be met.

Hence the preferred status here,
the macrame and wooden beads;
a chance to lounge in inner offices.

It creates an ambiance; we increase the bar tab
for the pleasure of an extra stick
of celery in some poor sap's Caesar.

Talk to it in hushed tones
of Wall Street argot then,
or pouty, lipsticked promises –

in shopping malls, above the
parquet floors, wherever music
is pumped in like a deadly gas.

Its new shoots will nuzzle air
the way a violin player does
his previous leaf-curled Stradivarius.

Moses-in-the-Cradle (Oyster Plant)
(Rhoeo spathacea)

First Moses, then three-men-in-the-boat;
to wit, their sexy bits suggest nothing better
or more savant than good old homo sapiens;

no bud more apt to steer their peerage out of reeds
and offbeat foliage than the green glans of some
pecker-up-to-the-neck in male metaphor?

It seems odd. Odder still some amateur botanist
should liken them to the oyster without seeing pearls –
unless his mind was in the gutter or scudding shore.

Every since Tennyson's rudder got stuck in the mud
it has been boats; every thought has pitched and tossed
three men over peak and trough in tub or collander

to get here. So pretty soon it will be Oyster and
Ben Wa Balls. Something in the way of sexual aids
to point the way to their green shade; and for every

pea green boat they'll send up strapping great hosannas,
blush pink and purple underleaf – so we'll suppose.
They'll row, row, row our retinal boat right off the sill.

V

LEARNING TO BREATHE

-1992-

Another Hansel And Gretel Story

1. Prologue

Which summer is it, your tenth, eleventh?
I'm two years older, still young enough to
squeeze through the hole in the same fence.

Smell of juniper, a well-barbered hedge
gives way to rot, old rusty nails.
Oak leaves crackle like small autumn fires
beneath bare potatoes of elbows and knees.

We are brothers, goad each other through
more than elbows and knees of our old clothes.
Innocence by now is a scuffed pair of shoes;
the teacher's apple is both battered and bruised.

Cigarette butts litter the clearing. These
spent cartridges, fresh packs potent
as new ammunition. The nudie photos
wait, rolled up, in old mason jars.

Our fort's a dam of negative space
formed by beating back bush and thorns
into an igloo-shaped hollow, a place
in which to hide, lob words against

the terrible silence of smouldering desire.
We salute large breasts, men's stroke book
visions of split, dewy mons, resplendent
pink flesh, lace, garters, the very first

burning bush ever to spring
from light lovely Lycra! Amazing!
Wondrous as any pink-eyed white rabbit
we ever flushed from that dark wood

or have hidden since, tamped back
into the glass jars, stuffed down
a threatening round barrel or hole.

2.

Strain your ears. Can you hear?
Upstairs. Mom and Dad making love.

The night is a dark cowl, a hood
we stretch over our furless backs.

Closer. The sound of our hearts
kicking like frightened rabbits
long held by the nape of the neck.

In our hands the bunched up sheets;
memories balled like Kleenex,
rubber bulbs we hold, squeeze
in the sweaty palms of our hands.

❀ ❀ ❀

Go back further, turn thought infrared.
Catch the reclusive witch next door
bending over her smouldering couch.

Note the frantic, pale hand
scrabbling like a rodent smoked
out of her long coat sleeve.

See how she struggles
to beat out the long ash
that burrows deep into the pile.

Between her legs, rumour has it,
there once was a similar hole.
A girl her father could not flush out.

Now the tops of this old crone's nylons
swallow fat thighs the way two pythons
might swallow two transfixed little pigs.

What burned in her groin? What burnt out?
What bastard child, what deformed head
crowned there years ago no one must know.

3.

Death is a pet we bury in a shoe box,
a cross constructed of popsicle sticks
or an "x" of stones mother allows
to mark the spot in the back flower bed.
A brief respite in the ways of plastic soldiers
whose C.O. commands we disinter the bones.

Go back.
No skeletons; no bones.
Only crows, a flight of long days
with the last crumb of innocence in their
leader's beak. We fling handfuls of pebbles,
watch the crows circle back.
We pick up feathers, run fingers over them,
knit them together the way mother
does for us, always checking the zippers
of our worn, patched khaki corduroys.

Turtles, goldfish, hamsters, mice,
a canary once: all gone, buried like toys.
Evil's only an afterimage of a magazine
monster, projected in full-frontal spread,
a luminous skull of rumpled white sheets
at the foot of the bed.

4.

We see the old hag burning
tires in the backyard.
A black plume rises from
the burned-out bunkers
of her eyes.

It is a small town,
another country,
another time.

Each tire sends up sparks.
They flit like small birds
in the highest branches of the tree.

She is looking out from a dark wood
to where her village once stood.

Her head sits like an owl, grips
the branch of an old oak.

Any moment now mice will
emerge from the rubble,
skitter into the clearing.

Talons will find fur
as the five tines of her fork
stir through the ash.

5.

Ten or eleven. Memory a long line
of breadcrumbs through the dark woods.
Dog-chewed plastic soldiers, dinky toys
surface where bones might have been.
It is difficult to remember the time scheme.
Movies: **Pork Chop Hill** and The Longest Day
envelop us, extend their blue pseudopodia
from the T.V. screen, our family's four walls.

A world of sin opens like some huge
sweet-smelling carnivorous plant.
Drowsy as bees caught in the sugar
of pop bottles we leave all day
on the front porch, we fall into it.
Become heroes and rogues both
anxious to try out the television roles.

Conscience is a lid we punch nail holes in.
Clap over the jar of the old lady's back yard
so she can breathe while we watch
her climb the glass sides of her own life.

✤ ✤ ✤

Now it is not **The Munsters, The Adams Family**
we hold up to the light; not a drowsy insect
careening around the narrow lip of a bottle
we see, but a father and daughter falling
over each other like bugs at the bottom of a jar.

❧ ❧ ❧

NO SOLICITORS, NO PEDLARS, NO NOTHING:
yellow paper affixed to the front door
by the big-headed thumbtacks of our eyes.
Which Halloween is it? The paper curls
like a dog's upper lip. Words scratch:
a German Shepherd behind a thin door.
We knock, knock again, because the old lady
will mutter and curse quite audibly,
but will never, ever open the door.

6.

Ritual demands a trip to the barn,
and so we must go there, one at a time.
If not to see what hangs from the rafters,
then to see the empty cages stacked high.

This, while the old woman is home,
we have witnesses who have been,
know the surge of long grass, rush
and kiss of flames at the heels.

This, while the moon is full, plump
as any white chicken in the hand of a geek,
or when it is thin, milky and
melts like wafer under the tongue.

❧ ❧ ❧

There is a dead cat:
curled, furless humunculus with
skin pulled thin as rice paper
over its foetal-bowed bones.

We lift it with a stick,
watch the maggots fall gentle
as rain drops from the full
eaves of its weathered ribs.

❧ ❧ ❧

Think now: was there
ever a foetus miscarried,
buried in the basement?

Could incest ever be uglier
than the rumour we let
past the white picket fence
of our perfect teeth?
Turn the cat over again.

7.

Lift the receiver,
the sound of the old bat's breathing
scurries like rats
single file down the wire.

Silence: an invisible,
colourless gas
tumbles from air vents,
seeps under the sash.

A huge darkness with
its sack of light
laughs up the chimney,
grins under the doors.

Gather brown flowers
from parks and boulevards.
Add water and stir
in a black patent purse.

Curse and jump the fence when
she comes at you with her car.
Yell across the years
your abject apologies.

Tell her you really
like her cookies
and you're truly sorry
for nibbling at her walls.

Pass her the hard,
brittle bones of your words;
tell you, if you can;
you're fat enough now.

8. Epilogue

And what of this gingerbread house?
After age and realtors come to call:
isn't there a sausage machine after all?
Do words not break our bones
to make their bread? Are lice
not crawling in her hair?
You stand and stare, and still
the words like moths eat
holes in the closet of old coats
that hang in open air.

Chicken bones are piled in a pyramid
in one corner of the livingroom floor.
Mouse turds tumble from all the cupboards.
Basin, tub, and tile turn the colour of autumn leaves.
Aquariums grow greener than the eyes of cats.
Chickens in canary cages look fatter than the day.
Are there no children in the oven then?

Your feet go through the floorboards
in all the basement rooms.
Where do we go then? What do we do
when all the words we speak are pieces of bread
torn from the same loaf; all the words we've spoken
are fat black birds that eat our way home?

Henry, In Mid-Leap

"Henry Lee has lost his wits.
Henry sucks his mother's tits,"
We kids would yell
until this hairy, gentle man
would take the bait and give chase,
run, shambling, ape-like, after us.

We would jump across a ditch
and he, faithful as a family dog,
would follow. Back and forth,
KA-nip KA-nop, a pingpong ball.
We would laugh; he would laugh.

So loving and trusting and gullible
he'd do it for hours if we let him
or he didn't fall in and get soaked.
For Henry Lee had lost his wits,
and his mother did love him so.

She'd call him for supper, and he
would come. A perfect loving son.
That is, until his mother died
and something of Henry broke inside.
Then he wouldn't let the girls touch
his big, hairy thing, or play with it.

Then there was no one left
to wind him up, take his hand,
or point his purple pecker home.
No relatives. No friends.
Just some men who were nice once
and gave him a ride in their van.

They took him to their castle-on-a-hill:
he escaped and found a bigger ditch –
a river wide enough and deep enough
to take him home. And Henry jumped
into a blue and cloudless morning,
believing he would catch us,
finally, on the other side.

Condom Tales

1

Times were so tough Wes used to wash out his condoms with a tooth-brush, hang them right there on the clothesline next to Sylvia's re-usable pads. "Party hats" he called them when the neighbours' kids would ask what they were, or "toques for the Pope's nose." Then snapped, "Now mind your business and go home."

2

The safe machine in the Dominion Hotel john offered a rainbow of colours to choose from, might have been a gumball machine, or so it must have seemed to some wise kid who etched "This gum tastes like rubber" next to the crack "Break one and win a baby!"

3

"Gossamer thin and smooth as silk" the label on the box used to read, meaning, I suppose, you'd scarcely notice the condom once it was on; but no; we noticed, and more than once withdrew with the pope wearing a droopish toque or, like Tom Terrific, went toot toot and blew a hole in the hat out of which issued great gouts of smoke that somehow indicated we'd got the idea, and hoped the ardent little spermatazoa would some-how fag out before they swam the channel and not get to shake the major's hand while the sunburst of fallopian fireworks gave back delayed rumbles to our ears.

4

And somewhere I read of a male pill. Developed and tested. Piloted years ago by willing inmates with high libidos and little to do but wank into tubes. It got the sperm count down all right; was abandoned nonetheless. Marketing problems; it didn't sit well with alcohol appar-ently, and so would never sell. The male body its own highball; so now we're just waiting for something to float the olives, while we twiddle, fiddle with the swizzle sticks.

5

Talk like brother plumbers of fittings and valves. Vasectomies seemed like such a good idea, so easy to work on outside plumbing and never mind what was hidden behind the drywall. The faucets and fittings were so well installed. We were pleased with the aesthetic of a single spout. Now we're back to re-plumbing our women too.

6

In order to purchase his first condom my brother had to buy one comb, one toothbrush, a bottle of aftershave, pay tax twice and return to the counter ten minutes after the large-breasted woman in Pharmacy was gone. Once he had the box of condoms in his hand and, seeing our father in nearby Stationery, had to ditch it on a shelf of shampoo. All this at a time when my younger cousin bought 12-cent comic books one at a time so he wouldn't have to pay the one penny tax.

So with the economics of sex. You had to make it with someone. But that someone had to appear to be a part of the weekly grocery bill: an item under Sundries. Love came in disposable lots. Something like the funny papers on Sundays: useful afterward for wrapping fish heads before we took them to the garbage cans.

7

The pill made it as easy for the man as putting coins in a parking meter and gave us all a meter to feed. Most of the women I went out with before I married were on it; making love together, we could almost hear the click click click of the biological clocks moving the needle in a clean sweep across the dial of our eyes. So hungry for whatever coin we could give each other. Ultimately one or the other of us would run out of spare change.

After thirty our women tell us there is nowhere to park your desire on the street. Everyone is circling the same few blocks. Looking for the perfect slot: one block from dinner and as close to the theatre as possible.

8

Now it could cost a man or a woman his or her life to have sex together. We wear them out of respect – something like dark clothes at a funeral, or asbestos suits in a house fire.

9

Some say the sexual revolution is dead. The singles bar has acquired the ambience of a church social, complete with little sandwiches. We all must take little bites, recite a new catechism of need. Confess indiscretions of the flesh.

Everywhere the lovers are breaking out hats. Placing them like serviettes next to the table. It's going to be a long feast or a famine. It's time to draw up our chairs and say grace. Get ready for the rich feast of binomials of genus and species. Set out the cutlery for loaves and fishes all over again.

Someone should invent industrial strength condoms. Condoms built to last: prophalactics with ziplocs that double as freezer bags. That way we might save ourselves from what we've become. We can approach each other from inside special gloves. Stay the radioactive isotope of love.

Poem After a Photograph in MOTHER JONES

So peaceful seem the severed heads,
so relaxed, so calm the almond eyes,
the pocked and blood-smeared cheeks;
so peaceful as to seem asleep,
to have dreamed themselves that way.

Any day the wind might blow,
riffle through the black fields
of their luxuriant, full-bodied hair,
and lift them from this abattoir soft
as soap bubbles from a child's breath,

and they will float for a while,
drift above the stippled stalk
of God's ragged dandelion clock,
settle, one by one, on El Salvador's
blood-engorged soil and sand.

They will send down roots that grow new
bodies whose arms and legs are safer
than the ones they remember having before,
bodies eye-deep in earth and blood
whose skulls grow nondescript as stones.

Beijing Massacre

To be in Tiananmen Square that day
was to be one drone in a hive of bees,
one leaf shaking, bending away
from a strong headwind in a tree.

The country lay still as a man
with bees in his beard,
until the bees became beard,
the beard a single cluster of bees
gathered around a pheromone
of hope and of fear.

The country became one man
covered from head to foot
in a cluster of bees,
the one man's thought
devoted to the idea
of learning, once again,
how to breathe.

And the bees' one thought:
how to breathe with him,
how to collapse and swell
like a bellows to feed
one man the oxygen he needs.

How to retain the shape of the man
when the man's body depends
like a ripe plum from the tree.

When what a plum wants
with all its being
with the fullness of time
is to ripen, to fall,
and to be eaten.

When all it needs
is the heat of the sun
and a little gravity,
one mouth to open,
to say "plum"
once, perfectly,
and taste it
on its tongue.

New Black Shoes

for Marika

Gangway grannies! Heads up grandpas!
Single moms with sullen broods in tow,
Christmas shoppers with coin slots for mouths
unstitch your brows, open Al Jolson eyes.

Marika's got new black patent leather shoes!
Is a bowling ball rolling clickety clack
down the mall. Nothing short of a potted palm
will stop her. She smiles in each shiny toe.

She doesn't need to click her heels thrice
and repeat "There's no place like home"
to get from Oz to wherever she's going,
and this sure as hell ain't Kansas!

Planets, whole galaxies of Christmas lights
gleam back from those toes. "I'm Dorfy, Mom.
I'm Dorfy!" she exclaims. Look at me go!
The wizard, whatsisname's got nothing on me.

So who cares if he's off on a coffee break
and none of his photo-taking elves are on seat.
This ain't Ox or the North Pole, but I've got
black patent leather shoes. I'm Dorfy. I'm me.

Shhh, They're Sleeping

The old Singer had not been used
for anything but a plant stand
when our daughter commandeered it.
Now its six little drawers are crypts,
Murphy beds for dinosaurs.
The Stegosaurus sleeps in one,
The Tyrannosaurus Rex in another,
Triceratops in a third, and so on:
each carefully molded out of play dough
and left to fossilize in Kleenex swaddling.

A nice touch is the short strings she ties
to each little knob, the switchboard
linkage from one drawer to another.
Now it's as though a telephone operator
had given us a direct line from Plasticene
to Pleistocene. We not only share
a planet's reserves of bondable carbon atoms,
but a party line with the crusty old folds
of the Upper Cretaceous. Shhh, Marika says
whenever we stray too close. They're sleeping.

On a molecular level, we like to think
she may be right. Who knows what sediment
the fluorocarbon layer and exhaust emissions,
spent fossil fuels, and paving are laying down
in the form of fallout from recombinant atoms?
All we can do is pussyfoot around the playroom.
Listen to the roots of each potted plant
as they suck up nutrients like the last
quarter-inch of some teenager's vanilla shake.
Tramp down years of sediment everywhere we walk.

Telefomin Trousers

for Don & Susan Low

Whoever thought of the name
had his head screwed on right.
Imagine the ad campaign
that could be built around
these two alliterative words:
"All the best Third World people
are wearing them this season ...
Feel the sea breeze in your hair,
let it caress your derriere."

The four syllables of the adjective
suggest a picturesque village
in the Shetlands or Orkneys,
some Atlantic rookery
buffeted by wind, celebrated for
the fine homespun wool
of its dour-faced sheep.

Telefomin. Telefomin ...
You can hear a thick brogue,
practically see some old guy's
moustache come up dripping with foam
as he bangs the table with his
empty pint of Guinness
or Thistle brand stout.

Aye, and there lies a tale
in the choice of noun too.
So proper, so serious:
we're talking British flannel here –
By Appointment to Her Majesty,
the Queer Old Dean. Designer label
in a pair of Carnaby slacks
with creases so sharp
they could slice cheese.

But no. These trousers are not
tailored from the finest wool
or polyester dacron,
but are grown; nay, grow wild,
are hand-picked from the vine
in Telefomin, New Guinea,
and aren't trousers at all!

Indeed, if I wasn't told otherwise,
I would have thought these
Peter pan gourds with their
elfin curlicue tips were
powder horns, or at least
were used to store some
aphrodisiac or herbal emetic.
The thong of binder twine glued
beneath the thatched band of grass
might be worn over the shoulder.

Instead, this thingamabob is worn
over the penis. The binder twine
fits around the waist;
the gentle curve of the gourd
is worn up, between the legs,
like Peter Pan's winkle pickers
or Alladin's Scheherazade slippers.
Thus, there is no need of guessing
the extent of a man's wealth.

You have to laugh when you think
of grown men traipsing around the jungle
like that. With not a stitch on
but their Telefomin Trousers. You do
when you tell me the tale. I do
as I gaze in amazement at the souvenir
on my study wall. And yet a man might
liberally sprinkle a kind of moondust
from this little cornucopia too.

Imagine the men of our society
wearing them instead of pants.
How the Peter Pan curve might restore
a kind of innocence to members
that long to poke their heads
over waistbands like Kilroys
with wide eyes and little "o" mouths.
And think then of the codpiece:
the cup that made much ado of nothing
and hid whatever the little guy
kept tucked inside his leotards.

Maybe if Adam had been issued
a pair of Telefomin Trousers,
Eden would not have become
a designer or sex boutique
but something more akin to
a trick and joke shop
where you might buy condoms
that fit like a night cap
instead of the nylon stocking
or ski mask a cat burglar wears.

All our men – dingled or donged –
could pretend to be Peter Pan,
and take Wendy and the kids –
with or without nightshirts
out the bedroom window
for a spin around the neighbourhood.
We could stud our Telefomin Trousers
with beadwork and jewels,
instead of our scabbards.
We could put up our bright swords.

Think of it! In less than a decade
we might replace the points of our missiles
with delicate curves. The older they are
the more curved we could make them;
ram's horns poking out of every silo,
great architectural thing poems that followed
the aesthetic of the Fibonacci sequence
and sat there for all to wonder at
like Nautilus shells dragged from
some briny deep of the unconscious.

Even men's penises might evolve into
sea cucumber-like organs, party favours
that ended in a feathery flick
instead of a bald head and Simonized shine.
Might come alive, mouths agape
like birds in their nests,
rather than rise like heat-seeking missiles
from silos deep beneath hopsack or denim.
If only we wore Telefomin Trousers,
trained our little pickles
to stretch for the light.

VI

FROM THE MOUTHS OF ANGELS

-1993-

Improvisation For Two Hummingbirds

1.

A fine pair you are! You hover
over our apple tree, dart in,
out of green leaves: swift hands
rummaging through bargain basement
colours, a profusion of pants,
slightly damaged red sleeves.

Dame Nature, handy with a needle
and thread, and an old hand
at stitching brand-name labels
on a tatty pair of genes, could
do no better in stitching up time.

2.

Knowing you are attracted to red
the way a pair of old boozing buddies,
old rummies on the dole are
to any mark, we watch you
hone in on the multifoliate flowers,
the freshly-laundered shirts.

You hang exclamation marks in the air.
We bang this tube of artificial colour,
sucrose and water. Spring a Kool-Aid
plasma bag with an invisible, intravenous drip,
a cold Heperin lock latched on an old apple bough.

3.

Addicts deprived, you spy the cheap
cherry extract left at eye-level.
A bottle on a shelf in a grocery aisle.

Long bills probe the collapsed blue vein
of winter's old wizened arm,
until you hit the mainline.
Light flags ruby red
on the hard edge of air.

Feathers glisten, turn iridescent with
the rush we feel on this side of the glass.

4.

Such a thrill! Four red plastic bells blare:
concert bullhorns proclaiming the news
while you hang clean, clear soprano notes
all about the tree, or blister thirty-second
notes, arpeggios East, West, North, and South,
fly like Tyner across all the old keys.

Such genius! To dip into the grill cloth,
steal the electricity right out of the wires!
This beats Hockey Night In Canada,
the huge quadraphonic video of instant replay.
Such an improvised buzz, your wings' soft focus
outdoing Manet, picking up passion's petitpoint
with more precision, more expertise than Seurat,
flitting among leaves, tongue flicks, pure acetylene!

Lovebird

after Percy B. Shelley's
"To A Skylark "

Hail to thee!
Poop 'n' Squawk,
peach face, old knob!

Say something! Come on!
Don't just gnaw on
that sandpaper perch!

Poke your head
out of the cage!
Make a break for it

and fly the gamut of perches
in this clapboard joint!
Squawk metaphor for all you're worth!

(Seventy five bucks at least)
The carpet is green if nothing else.
It's not curtains yet, there chump.

Chin up! Eat my art prints,
shit on my books, if it
will make you any happier.

The old girl's gone. Egg-bound.
Kaput. There is nothing you
can do but hang ten

off the gang plank,
jump into the flurry
of air's atoms now.

Natter your dismay at
the squadron of chickadees
on the other side of the glass

if you have to
while I peck at the keys
behind my own paper arras.

71

We're all flying assholes. Poop,
and that, my fine-feathered friend,
is the sad nub of it all.

Wind whistles blue skies
through all our damn bones.
Why stop half way down the dark shoot?

Amadeus Macaw

Six days and a shriek
tears through the green silk
of dream: I'm on the phone
to your owners again;

watch as you play out
the aristocratic spool
of your blue-blooded gyre.

You eat pine needles now,
chew bitter bark from
strange evergreens nearby.

Wind down the spiral
of golf courses and forest,
suburban streets in search

of a mate. Poor Amadeus.
Only the crass caw of crows,
the plebeian titter of finches
answer your cry today.

It's cold. All too soon
the sky will betray you
with its denuded trees
and stippled gooseflesh.

You will have to return
or fly through the eye
of winter's long needle.
Both ends of our binoculars

train on a troubled red bird
in your maker's blue eye.
There are no Amazons perched
on the sleeve of this day.

Like a tonearm your
silhouette comes back,
drops into dark grooves
to play all the blue-green
cadenzas of escape and pain.

From The Mouths of Angels

One day there are four mouths to feed,
the next time you look there are only two,
a scrawny hatchling hangs, feet caked
in dung, body glistening, depending
from the nest like a wet line of drool.

Mum's the word from these butterballs
on the fate of the fourth. Sky's a shrug,
the ground nappy with unfettered green,
sports only boutonnieres in its buttonholes.
No grief here, Jack! No kwashiokor bellies
straining atop outsized, weak bandy knees.

Gone the concertina ribs and stump wings!
The portly survivors wheeze, inflate
graciously in their ill-gotten, satin Diors.
Could as easily belch caviar, cough
from a habit of the best Havanas
as go into peristaltic conniptions
over any mere regurgitated worms.

They're not in a flap to go anywhere
either. Regard you with eyes
as dull as galvanized roof nails,
down-turned Edward G. Robinson mouths.
No more suspicious, seedy, or shifty
than any toady couple flush enough
to afford this seat in the loges. They watch,
wait for you to let go of the drapes.

The Tallest Totem

(with apologies to Margaret Hurdon Keifer)

1.

Familiar Kilroys of the times,
the highrise apartments peak
above Beacon Hill's garden treeline
as only eyes and noses might:
nosy bourgeois neighbours parting
Emily's preternatural green drapes.

2.

Outstripped in height by far,
the tallest totem is nonplussed,
if not defiant of the white man's ways:
still the tallest totem – recently raised
five feet to keep up with competition –
it raises a stiff middle finger in salute.

3.

At night the lighted windows
like a thousand highlights
in the ice cube of a single drink
radiate dazzling affluence:
a toast to the sunset of our days.

4.

The tallest totem reaches out,
its shadow stretching like a pool cue.
Lines up the moon and stars
for the challenge of the table,
banks our eyes off the nearest horizon
into a side pocket of homespun truth.

Quick's Bottom

Time now to build a new fence.
This hemistich of trees
is insufficient to peg
the unused blue flap of sky.

Barbed wire, old cedar posts
lean at snaggletooth random.
The horizon's raw, inflamed
as old pyrorrheic gums.

A wizened jack-o-lantern
guttering on its own half light,
sun teeters on the sill of sense,
its mouth puckered around October's straw.

Hawthorns can't contain the truth
any more than the sharp spikes
of words can hold the writhing
translucent grub of the moon.

Everywhere post holes, footprints
well up like wounds behind us.
Colour returns to the sky
like blood to a white knuckle
where the land has let go.

VII

FLYING COFFINS

-1994-

(Nigeria 1980-82 / Canada 1982-92)

The World According To Reuter

In Kigali, the capital of Rwanda,
government officials have announced
the official bride price will be
three hoes instead of the traditional cow.

Mothers with daughters of marriageable age
are outraged and claim, indignantly,
this devalues the worth of a young girl to
less than the price of a basket of bananas.

Yet more injurious than the blow
to the haughty parents' pride
is the considerable loss in carrying charges,
the attack on small business growth.

Some fathers have been known to command
100,000 Rwandan francs (about $1,640)
for making the beast with two backs
spit out the right genetic code –

and there is no denying they work at it.
Like zealous patrons at the slot machines
in Vegas or Maseru or Macao
they pump their women full of small change.

Until three sour lemons light up their eyes
and the women spill forth babies! babies!
Babies that become sons with strong wills;
babies that become daughters with strong backs.

And while many young people approve
of reducing the bride price to a nominal gift,
the stalwarts of the ruling National Revolutionary
Movement for Development party strongly object.

They would as soon move cows, move their bowels
as cave in to the practice of tilling their
daughters' wombs for the price of a few hoes.
Their minds slam shut cash register drawers.

Development or no development, it is the will
of the village men to keep producing children.
If it is hoes they will get for their pains, O.K.
Let there be daughters. Let there be hoes.

Zavin, On The Night Shift

Ask him; he laughs about it now.
It was a Rock 'n' Roll war,
bang-bang-shoot-em-up
in the Muslim sector of Bierut;
an eight-hour day shift, a job.

Afterward, he and his buddies
would knock off, retreat
to the Christian side for pizza,
change their clothes, clean up
and maybe go out dancing.
This was the routine.

There were still plenty
of unshelled buildings
in the Christian quarter then.
Then a bullet grazed his temple;
he packed his bags and left.

Here, in Maiduguri,
venerable Muslim capital of Bornu,
he works with Arab bosses
and Nigerian day labourers,
is foreman for a Nigerian/Lebanese
steel and engineering firm.

Now he inspects rivets,
oversees the welding of
school desks and building trusses.
Weekends, spends himself
in the lithe black bodies
of Cameroonian whores he says
drain his spuds and ask for more.

One woman in particular,
given her druthers, chooses him;
sometimes gives him "long time,"
does things – special things –
sometimes just to be with him,
and they've become friends.

All night, every two weeks or so,
he looks for her. Ask him.
She's good to him and knows his kinks.
Together they make a truss
of their uneasy nonpartisan lust.
All night he shoots his rivets into her.

Upside-down Tree

Stark ganglions of nerves teased, razed from the burnt flesh of earth – said by the Kanuri to grow upside-down in punishment for an unweaned pride: you were once the most beautiful tree in the world. Your trunk was as sturdy as ten elephants, your branches as supple as the limbs of Fulani servant girls. You carried the sun high as a hod of the most perfect mortar, light thickening, turning sweet as palm wine even as it spilled from the broken calabash of sky all around you. Embraced even the wild mongrel bitch, thin-ribbed, skittish eater of offal, and offered her shade.

Flies moved in a bellows at her scabious, worried ears, and still your shadows tickled her underbelly. You were kind if too beautiful after all, and many a lover would creep through the guinea corn to lie next to you. The hoopoe, with its crazy, zigzag flight, moved freely as a seamstress among your branches; weaverbirds made beautiful little grass purses for you to snap each day in like a single gold coin. But you were too full of yourself, too brazen for even the gods to ignore, and they punished you. Wrapped you first in a shroud of sand, hair shirt of harmattan, until you fell to your knees, pressed your forehead to the east. Such was your purdah. Then the dogs ripped the underbelly from the moon, ran, teeth gnashing at bitches in heat, until even their own tails could not curve round far enough to protect their own vulvas. And the gods ripped you up by the roots and inverted you. Forced each pouting stoma of your leaves to eat dirt. Held you under the sand as a farmer holds a bag of kittens under water in a barrel under the eaves.

Wilfulness suddenly runneling heavy rains until you slumped, breathless in their hands. Now we think: how like a god to invent images of such penury: how like the heart's dendritic branches to hang its thieves in pods, while light like thought seeps ever underground to seek its deepest shade. Upside-down tree, baobab, even if you wear bells on your feet and dance a dervish dance across the sahel now, there is no forest so dense the impoverished heart won't make it a desert, for the wind comes with daggers in its teeth. Still, you dance. Salome, Shiva with too many limbs for even a god to lop off. And swing the sun's head by its own gory locks.

VIII

WISER PILLS

-1995-

Dick and Jane Have Sex

Dick wants Jane. Jane wants Dick. They want it. Uh, uh, uh.

Dick lives with his Mom and Dad. Jane lives with hers. The trick is for Dick to find a way Jane can come out to play. The trick is for Dick to find a place. Look, Dick, look. Jane does not like brambles up her ass. Where can Dick and Jane be alone? Where can they be comfortable for the time it takes?

Dick drives a '55 Austin A-50 sedan. It is all he can afford. Too bad, Dick. It's too difficult here, even with the doors open. Dick and Jane know. They've tried it here before. In the front seat is a big steering wheel. The three-on-the-tree stick shift always gooses Dick. Uh, uh, uh. The back seat? Too narrow. Jane puts one big leg up on the back seat. One big leg up on the front. Still no good. Dick's Tyrannosaurus Rex arms scrunch up against his chest. Dick cannot fondle Jane's breasts.

See Dick sigh. Sigh, Dick, sigh. See Jane look up at the sky. Look, Jane, look.

Now Spring has come. Dick and Jane can walk the dog. Come, Spot, come. Wag, wag, wag. Dick has found a lovely glade. A hogfuel path where joggers run. Run, Spot, run. Doggies do their business here. Watch your step, Dick. Watch your step, Jane. Hurry up, Spot.

Dick ties Spot to a tree. Stay, Spot, stay.

"I love you," Dick says, and Jane takes off her panties. "I love you too, " Jane says, and Dick pulls out a safe. Together Dick and Jane put Dick's safe on baby Dick. Baby Dick sits up straight. Stay, Dick, stay. Dick squeezes the air out of the nipple reservoir. This act reminds Jane of putting up wallpaper. No. Of burping the Tupperware before putting leftovers back in the fridge. Ick, ick, ick.

Eventually, the logistics are taken care of. Dick kisses Jane. Kiss, kiss, kiss. A couple of gouramis. Dick sticks to Jane. Jane sticks to Dick. Dick fondles one of Jane's breasts. Fondle, fondle, fondle. Dick is a paraplegic, trying to strengthen his grip. Jane's breast is a rubber ball.

Dick licks Jane's breast. Dick licks the other breast. Around the aureoles goes his tongue. Round and round each nipple equally. Now this one, now that one. In smaller and smaller circles. Just like a tether ball, getting closer and closer to the pole. Oh, oh, oh. Now his tongue has wrapped around this one. Now it has wrapped around that one. Now a playful nibble. For this one and that one. Hard nipples, like maraschino cherries. Mmm good.

Jane for her part licks Dick's ears. Dap, dap, dap, goes her sweet little tongue. Just like a finishing brush around the delicately fluted molding of each one. Her pointed little tongue probes. Now inside his ear, now out. Jane is painting the window of Dick's soul and doesn't want to miss a spot. Her breath is hot on Dick's skin.

So hot Dick moves on. Follows Jane's lead. Pretty soon he is painting her tummy in long even strokes. Moves his tongue up and down her tummy. And daps at her belly button. Tee hee hee.

Oh, oh, oh, Jane groans and rocks from bun to bun to get more comfortable. Dap, dap, dap, goes Dick's tongue. Now along her hip bones. Carefully around her pubis. Slowly, carefully, probing lower. Parting the hairs of her bush like a little boy hunting golfballs. Deeper and deeper, probing the cleft of her mons. Deeper, parting the lips of her vagina. In and out and up, until Dick's nose is rubbing her pubic bone. And now like Spot in his dinner bowl. Round and round. Up to his ears in pleasure. Rooting, rooting for her clitoris. Spot chasing a gopher as far down a hole as his nose will go.

Until his tongue gets tired. Until Dick decides it's time. And Jane guides baby Dick like the nozzle of a hose into the gopher hole. To chase the gopher out some other orifice maybe. Her every arching pore perhaps. And Dick feeds himself to Jane, inch by slow inch, easing his glans over the lip of some mysterious well. Dropping the bucket of his will inside her, hand over hand. And Jane arches her back and cups Dick's buttocks to take all of him inside her. And Dick hums Jane. Hump, Dick, hump.

And Dick's buttocks glisten in the moonlight. "Oh, oh, oh," Jane moans. "Uh, uh, uh, " Dick grunts. "Ooo, ooo, ooo," Spot whimpers. Spot is not having fun. Spot wants to play too.

See Spot lurch. See Spot strain at the leash. His face just like Dick's. Big carotids bulging. "Ooo, ooo, ooo."

"Oh,! Oh! Oh!" Jane exclaims in falsetto accompaniment.

"Uh, uh, uh," Dick replies in rut, thrusting his proud penis home. Hump, Dick, hump. Uh – uh –wha-? What's this? Strange titillation. The feathery flick of canine tongue between his buttocks. Oh! Oh no! Dick cannot come. Jane sounds like a record. First on 78. Then like someone pulled the plug.

No. Spot, no! Don't hump Dick! Get up, Dick! Quick! Stay, Spot, stay! Baby Dick's gone droopish. Suffers post nasal drip. Dick still wants Jane. Jane still wants Dick. Spot just grins. Grin, Spot, grin.

Frank's Aquarium

It's been a bad day –
a bad stretch of days,
if you want to know the truth.
Frank doesn't want to watch the news –
anything else – this new British comedy –
the best thing on anyway – will do.

Workmen's compo cheque hasn't come,
the doctors won't tell him what's wrong
with the metal in his leg. He can't walk –
bones in his hands have to be re-set too.
Pretty soon the remote control will be
too tough to operate; he'll have to get up.

Well, shit, it hurts, eh? And the wife, she's
half the damn problem – having to come back
to Canada. To this unemployment, to this dive.
Not like the old days snorting coke, crystal:
deviating the old septum; making hay
painting houses of the rich in San Diego.

He had a big house then. Thought nothing
of spending money on really good dope –
not this shitty homegrown. Seems that
now he's in the slow lane, doing less
damage to body and soul, the shit comes
to him: his is the first shoe to find

the Saint Bernard's three-coiler on the lawn.
Trigger fish is even eating the new salt
water plants he bought the other day.
And six fish – six out of eight –
the most expensive ones, of course –
have bought the farm, bit it on account

of the copper solution for the lousy wrassie's
scale spots. Or maybe the new gravel
is to blame for that – stirring it up could
have increased the sulphate ion content
or buggered up the pH of the water – what with
all the shuffling of coral chunks and scenery.

No compo and the landlady on his back
for the rent in spite of the damage deposit
she's got in her hands. That, and all the damn
work he's done around the place, the lack
of a promised paint job and general
refurbishing – or wash and wax for the roaches.

You want to wish him luck or maybe
buy him the best damn piranha money
will buy, a half side of lean ground beef
to feed it, before there is a baby to feed
or his wife puts out and puts on the crotchless
panties he's bought. He plugs into her like

a video cassette. But right now you'll
wait outside the Chinese grocer's in
a Sikh, a Mennonite, a bible-belt town
while he takes back the plastic-covered magazine
that disallows the lady's little fish of a finger
exploring its own extruded, painted pink labia.

Sit and wait – your ears backed up with
enough of your own soft soap to foam, overflow
the mind's mad Maytag and watch the cars
slip by, scull awhile like fish in their
own polluted streams. For the moon is bright,
whiter than white panties hung on a line.

Frank's painted the back of the tank blue.
Bought a whole new quarantine tank –
to accommodate anything else that will keep moving
like leucocytes around his father's veins,
the metastases clouding the old rheumy eyes.
Frank's eyes dart like minnows from skirt to skirt.

He's broke. His sisters too – lazy shits – won't
lift a finger to help the old lady around the house.
One's on welfare; the other's a little slow – not slow
enough to stay off the streets – little cock tease.
You think of the little fish in one of Frank's books –
the ones that stay close to the big urchins' spines.

They'll gather around a six-inch spike like
it was a may pole or something – until you put in
something that's got two sticking out. Smart fish:
they at least know how to survive. Now you take
those high school girls: they know a good thing too;
as long as I'm holding, they'll bounce on my bed.

I'm not as bad as I used to be … he says.
Used to be the first hippy in my high school –
Ridgemont High – the place they shot the film –
That was after my time. Got busted in Mexico,
spent more time than I care to think about there.
Later, cops chased me right out of Huntington Beach.

The folks sent me up here to dry out.
I guess it worked. Funny though how shit sticks
to you when you're clean. I had more money and sex
than I knew what to do with down there; I did.
Now a woman points so much as a finger near her
pussy, they paint it over. We should make a video.

You want to suggest filming the tank. Recall
a line in Atwood's **Edible Woman** where the antagonist,
watching his clothes spin in a dryer, adds a pair
of green socks. He wouldn't have to change the water;
he wouldn't need new equipment. He could watch the fish,
his father's cargo of antibodies capsizing on screen.

That's it. Frank! Ambient imagery; eidetic fish.
A three-ring retinal circus! For every midden of cracked
shells, a moray or tentacle draped like a string
of pearls from some young woman's spread legs!
Breasts pressed like gorged anenomes against the glass!
You, gourami-like, groping among crinoids, parting white thighs!

Tell your wife to throw away the sexy lingerie she
thinks you bought to cover her up. Project the imagery
on the white wall where the headboard would be.
Enter her in the spirit of Lloyd Bridges, a
Jacques Costeau, exploring the briney deep.
See, the pubic hair grows lush as algae over everything.

The new sensurround is wonderful, isn't it?
Colour dots hum like a pointillist hive of busy bees.
Royal Jelly's rammed down each pampered pupil
and hormones leap like fish from every passing pink
stream of electrons, gather like iron filings around
the magnetic poles of wet T-shirts in every bar.

Cancer is just another concretion, a colonial reef
living off some hard centre that is already dead:
these polyps you fix on are enlarged sweat glands.
Will they drain off enough honey when your Father's dead?
Will your wife's small breasts bud off enough of the pain?
How long will you travel below the bubbles of your breath, Frank?

You'll have enough to do to keep the glass clean,
words' tiny radulae rasping away to clear a path
to the errogenous zones: you a Bob Guccione in pith helmet
hacking breasts like fungi off every green tree.
It's a losing battle, Frank. For every face they peel off
in the jungles down south, another goes on like a decal up here.

Howard's Teeth

Howie's got a theory about dental care
that fits right in with his proclivity
for five bottles of Coke a day,
and being a man of the woods,
can point out a lot of natural precedents.
The beaver, for instance: now there's
a creature that needs strong, healthy teeth.

And what colour are they? A dingy yellow,
even orange. And did you ever see a beaver
lose an incisor to a tree trunk? Not likely.
The thing is, you only get cavities if you brush:
if you don't bother, the scum builds up.
You end up with a hard, protective layer.

His plan is to leave his teeth alone as long as he can.
A fencepost theory. Leave them until they get soft,
begin to rot, then have 'em all hauled out
and replaced with false choppers. It's cheaper
than throwing good money after bad spot-filling 'em
when they eventually have to go anyway, he says.

He's going to get married in a year; let him
worry about 'em then. In the meantime, there's
the sweet taste of Coke, and he nurses
a single bottle for better than an hour.
Coke and cigars give his mouth a familiar
feel of compost, and he never has to eat words.

Making An Angel for Bob

It's my first real job –
after summers of picking strawberries
and mowing lawns. I've already failed
as a would-be waiter by slopping tea
in saucers and customers' laps,
sweated or smelled too strongly of Brut
to ever make maitre d' material.

So I'm happy to be a stockboy
helping Bob stamp packets of Jello gelatin
and listen, wrapt withal, as he explains
the intricacies of maintaining stock
on the shelves of his section.
I have a red apron,
am discharged with a grave responsibility,
to hear Bob describe the job.

He's not all there, but never mind;
his shock of red hair and Coke-bottle lenses
give off an aura of immense concentration,
and, right now, I am his understudy,
there is much I must learn. Bob is intent
on getting twenty little boxes of cherry Jello
into the empty space between lemon and orange.
Cherry always sells out first, he says;
you've got to watch it closely.

A kind of awe comes over me. I might
be watching the best safecracker in the business
turn the tumblers that will open the boss,
Henry Eng's very own vault. Only Bob's
lost it. His hands begin to shake
and packets of Jello tumble from the shelves.
Forty-five boxes – one for every year of his life –
fall in slow motion, split, spill
a rainbow of coloured crystals onto the floor,
and Bob can't take it today. Hurls his stamp
into the shelves and jumps all over the Jello boxes
until not a single one is left uncrushed.

Then, nonplussed, Bob suddenly stops,
runs his fingers through his shock of hair
to train it into place. Gently, deliberately,
unties his green apron, lets it drop,
and spins on his heel to leave.
The Jello sparkles like virgin snow.
I want to get down on my back
and move my arms and legs
with calisthenic precision,
make an angel for Bob.

Big Al's Trick

Big Al's got less then five years to go
before he retires. Put a lot of years in
running his own orchard in the Okanagan
before he ever got here. Now a charge hand
on Grounds for the local school board,
he does as little as he has to in summer,
and like a ground hog who never shows
his shadow, makes for the boiler room
every chance he gets all winter long.

To drive with Al is a pleasure
because he always takes his time.
And when you get where you're going,
he will tell you clearly what to do,
pick up a few pebbles from the parking lot,
then take off a shoe. The pebbles lend
verisimilitude to this trick, of course,
and it's uncanny how he always manages
to be on his feet emptying that shoe
whenever the boss comes around.

Yet every weekend he puts in overtime
selling things he's bought at garage sales
from a table in the Swap and Shop.
For Big Al is nobody's fool
and knows his junk. And every Monday,
as sure as God made little green apples,
both his shoes are worn and scuffed.
See. He holds one in his hand, turns it over
and over, as if looking for a blemish
in a perfect autumn windfall; weighs it
carefully, smiles at the heft of it,
before gently setting it down on the lawn.

Not by Chinny Chin Chin

Four a.m. A sudden screech
drives my wife out of bed.
Shifting and grinding of gears,
gunning of a truck engine,
repeated crunch of metal on cement ...?

Sure enough: our neighbour's pick-up.
Damn fool husband's drunk again.
Only this time he's flying on some
high-octane fuel, something that's
compressed all his rage into the crazy
detonations of six re-bored cylinders.

A bull that has long since forgotten
what red flag got him pawing,
snorting at the ground in the first place,
he is attempting to gore his own front door
with a six-foot rack of checkerplate.
Charges across the front lawn,
up his own steps again and again.

Toro! Toro! Something in his head commands,
and he lowers his center of gravity,
attacks the foundation of all common sense.
And to think that over here the closest
we get to this sort of thing is to read
The Three Little Pigs to our kids.

How to tell them the man next door
is not the big bad wolf, his three kids
are not Fiddler Pig, Fifer Pig, and Practical Pig
I do not know. But the way they look
at what goes on in our backyard
has me wondering about
their house of sticks and our brick house.

Did the guy's wife finally get fed up
with his drinking and carrousing
and kick him out? Did she have some
pot of oil cooking in the fireplace for him
when he came home? God only knows.
The children's eyes have the burnt-out look
of dying embers though. Sikokotok coals.

It's not because they're Native
I am afraid they will find matches.
I have already transmuted a bull
into wolf for the purpose of this tale –
was perfectly prepared to trade
in my own white liberal sheep skin
for the sake of the children.
It's that I don't want my own walls
to shake from some mad driver in my heart's
red crew cab. Not by my chinny chin chin.

Vasectomy

The decision was simple enough.
Sex isn't some funny uncle from Desmoines
who talks your ear off about plumbing
fixtures and valves, or harrumphs and egads
his way through hot tips of insider trading
while he puffs away at his dimestore cigar.

You can't console it with a back rub
or dusty old tin of Copenhagen snuff –
even if it promises you candy
or a shiny new silver dollar
for going to the store for it.

You are not a piggy bank
and it can't fill you up that way.
Nor is your body a parking meter
that can take pills like endless
rolls of quarters, and always be there
when you want to go out dancing.

We cannot expect lightning bolts from heaven
to light up the main circuit panel
then travel down the line
to some copper key kited high
inside your uterus either –
not without blasting the tree
to its very roots.

Love is not a shooting gallery.
There is no one to yell "pull,"
no guarantee every clay pigeon
will be hit by a perfect bullet,
even now when I plan on shooting blanks.
The target is not something you hit or miss.
You were not made from Adam's
or anyone's rib, as the fused halves
of my glans, the seam up
the shaft of my penis show.

The decision was simple,
something we could even be glib about;
it's easier to work on outside plumbing
than chase a knotted bit of cloth
with a snake throughout your pipes.

Just as we turn off the inside taps
so the water in the outside faucets won't freeze
and burst the pipes behind the drywall,
this little precaution with my spigot
steals a little juice from Peter
so we can afford to pay Paul.

Or say we are tending our garden, love –
pruning suckers from last year's roses
so they continue to bloom with promises.
Though our children grow apace,
we can find the garden again.
We need only tag a branch,
to find our old initials
still growing with the tree.

IX
NEW POEMS

The Canadian Guide To Death and Dying*

1. Comments on Doctors, Nurses, Hospitals, Autopsies, Funeral Homes, Cemeteries, Family and Bereavement

"I got no warning or information in the days before death. I would have appreciated contact with the doctors, or a phone call to indicate how serious the illness was."

Sometimes it's difficult to make the connection between Mr. Tsao's various attractions and his goal of death education. Practically the first thing I see after passing through the entry gate is a quarter-life-size statue of copulating elephants. A little farther into Happy Peace Garden I stare for some time at another artwork, trying to figure out what it is, until Mr. Tsao finally says, "Turtles." Indeed, a ten-times-life size statue of two turtles in flagrante delicto. Mr. Tsao puts sex and death together with the ease of a Hollywood producer.

"One of the staff members of the hospital told my son that his father would go to purgatory. I do not agree with this."

Besides hundreds of graves tightly packed together in rows going up the mountainside, among the other attractions is a lavish hundred-foot tower where relatives deposit their ancestors' remains after exhumation. In the lobby of the bone tower is the world's largest Chinese block with a hitting stick so big and unwieldy, Mr. Tsao has a standing offer of a thousand dollars to anyone strong enough to pick it up and belt the block with it.

"I asked the doctor in charge not to prolong his dying."

The final ... attraction is clearly Mr. Tsao's favorite, his equivalent of the Disneyland E ticket experience. It's called The Trip of a Lifetime (good name!) and is a moody tunnel that arches through the part of the hillside under the 750 Buddhas. Like any good theme park ride, the one-hundred-yard-long Trip takes its visitors through a story – in this case, the story.

"I would have liked relatives and friends to keep calling and visiting instead of staying away when they knew [the illness] was terminal."

At the top of the arch paintings suddenly turn quite graphic sexually, and I am enlightened and amused simultaneously. Eager heterosexual couples are depicted enjoying each other in a variety of positions: the elephant position, the turtle position, and so on. I ask Mr. Tsao if this is meant to be life's peak, the pinnacle of life's inevitable arch. He looks confused by the question, and finally says, "Top of the arch is not life's peak. It is just the top of the arch."

"A doctor should not turn his patient over to a strange doctor a week or two before the end. It's cruel."

The first thing His Highness did when he decided to become famous was build himself a bachelor apartment right at the heart of Precious Gold Mountain. It's a spectacular place, carved into the rock of the hill below all the graves. Large goldfish burble around in deep pools, water cascades down rock faces. (I do have a passing thought about where the source of the drinking water is. Let's see now, the graves are up there...)

"The funeral director was not dramatic, but practical. He explained all the costs."

Just as those high lamas who attend the Dalai Lama must ask his permission to die, so The Children's Television Workshop, Mr. Hooper's parents, also had to ask a higher authority for permission to shoot the Hoop. The authority they consulted was Research. CTW conducted extensive testing to determine how preschoolers would respond. They wanted to know whether Hooper Croak could be a "learning experience" or just something that scared the hell out of America's youth. Suitably bolstered by statistics and other data that confirmed mass tot trauma would not ensue, Hooper breathed his last long after actor Will Lee had done if for real. The actual episode was handled splendidly, with Big Bird once again assuming the role of Everytad.

2. Comments on Viewing of a Body

"I do not believe in elaborate funerals or in those teas they have after the funeral."

UNCLE HENRY: She got quite a bump on the head, we kinda thought there for a minute she was gonna leave us.

DOROTHY: But I did leave you, Uncle Henry, that's just the trouble!

—Noel Langley, **The Wizard of Oz** film script, 1938

❧ ❧ ❧

"When we die, neither of us wants the casket left open for others to look at."

And just ask the reptile dealer at the zoo which snakes are the biggest draw. It's the ones that can bring death with just the slightest nip. A reptile house without poisonous reptiles is a lonely place indeed, as lonely as Sea World without the killer whales.

3. Comment on Tissue and Body Donations

"This is a very useful idea, but I feel that the next of kin should decide."

4. Comments on Embalming

"The family arranged for the funeral without consulting me. It cost me more than twelve hundred dollars, not including the cemetery plot. I even had to pay for the flowers."

"We have two subjects today," Bob said to me when I returned to the mortuary itself. "One is a middle-aged, slightly obese male who I understand the cause of death was (sic) a hepatic liver condition, complicated by alcoholism (Max.) "Or we have a twelve-year-old girl who just came in. Which would you prefer to see embalmed?"

5. Comments on Bereavement

"Friends should let the widow talk instead of avoiding mention of her loss. Just talking helps."

❧ ❧ ❧

"Before, you were part of a couple. Now your whole scheme of life and living is different."

❧ ❧ ❧

"My life was their life, and now they both have passed away, I have nobody."

Practical Things You Should Know

A. Shipping a Body By Rail

"Shipping a body by rail may be complicated by the fact that changes are occurring in the railroad business. Many branch lines are out of use, and on open lines there may be no station master to accept a body for shipment."

B. Shipping a Body By Truck

"A body must be enclosed in a suitable box for shipping by truck. A flat rate must be pre-paid by the shipper. The rate of shipping a body by truck varies depending on the area, the transportation outfit, and the nature of their operation. Deterioration of any parcel shipped by truck is at the owner's risk."

C. Shipping a Body By Air

"Air Canada does not require that a body be embalmed for air freighting."

D. Parting With Such Sweet Sorrow...

"... in Ghana you can get a casket that looks just like a Mercedes with all the options. ...The Mercedes is the biggest seller amongst the standard Quaye designs, often purchased for or by a man who never had a Mercedes but certainly wanted to have one someday. And now he will have one all of his days. Other popular fantasy designs include elaborate boats for fishermen, rocket ships for kids, crabs for, I assume, crab catchers, various other assorted birds, animals, even insects. Mothers are often buried in large chickens, based on the Ghanaian proverb Akoko nan tiaba na enkum ba, which means 'The hen steps on its chicks but does not kill them.'"

Afterward: An Afterword

Two sweet old Unitarian ladies died, and as their souls ascended they came to a signpost hanging in the firmament. The signpost had two arrows, one pointing off to the right and one pointing off to the left. "This way to heaven," it said on the arrow pointing right. "This Way to a Discussion of Heaven" it said on the arrow pointing left.

They went left.

NOTE: This is a found text collage for several voices. Ideally, the voice in italics will be reminiscent of Robin Leach's narrator voice in

Lifestyles of The Rich and Famous; the other voices represent middle class Canadian carping about this and that, or making catty observations about the death arrangements of friends and neighbours – gossip and idle banter, replete with unexpected or unintended ironies. The voice of the Guide should be dry, pseudo scientific, and full of euphemistic understatement.

*All quoted material found in **The Canadian Guide To Death** and Dying by Jill Watt (Toronto, ON: International Self-Council Press, 1974); all material in italics extrapolated and quoted from **Death: The Trip Of A Lifetime** by Greg Palmer (San Francisco, CA: Harper Collins Publisher, 1993. The juxtapositions are my own. R.S.

The Embolism

for Susan

Your fifth dive,
surfacing from sixty feet.
You pull the J-valve
like a cork from a bottle.

I want to say champagne
bubbles are released,
the surface is
a hogshead of real fire,

the jinn in that cylinder
so cramped, so desirous
of its own freedom
you can only follow it,

but the world is indeed
too much with us,
and slaps you in the face
instead of on the bottom.

We too, sheath-wet
in our second skins,
stand upon the shore
like acolytes to greet you,

only the mist
from our masks
is not blue smoke
dispensed from censers,

and can keep nothing at bay
for all the susurration
of waves saying shh, shhh,
it's all right, it's O.K.

And nothing is
and nothing will be again,
for the man laying prone
flippers splayed

is no clown or seal
waiting his turn to jump
from drum to drum
through imagined flames,

and no Charlie Chaplin
whose pratfalls are endearing,
so safely taken in transfusion
up a black chord from a wall.

His fall from grace
the result of using his reserve
to descend rather than ascend,
of not following his jinn into space.

The kelp offshore writhe:
a den of snakes he should have
climbed over and not tried
to swim under with so little air.

Now sky pinches, a round
rubber seal that holds
your ruptured world at bay.
We bow heads and pray.

We must all look like fish
pressed against the glass
the thickness of two skins away,
our words so many bubbles rising…

But to what surface now?
There is no way we can get
the jinn back in the bottle,
let alone this man's burst lungs.

Waves lap against the shore,
each and every one of them
a draw sheet pulled taut
over your father's face.

Talking Back To Zoloft

How can you and I be friends?
Our relationship is ambivalent at best.
I spend quality time with you – every day –
at my wife's urging, and in truth,
you do help, do level out my moods.

You're cute too in your little fifty
mg, yellow and white bomber jacket,
and you take the curves en-route
to your destination with grace and elan,
never squeal your tires or lose the road.

You're expensive though and I
don't like to line the body men's and mechanics'
pockets, even if I can write you off
and get reimbursed for your
shenanigans and escapades.

And, make no mistake, you're
a fair weather friend, if that.
Sure, it's fun to motor along with you –
to take those crazy curves
at a hundred miles an hour.

I like the wind in my hair – I do.
And there's still enough of it that I
can affect a leonine mane and demeanor,
but my growl was always worse
than my bite and I don't need you –

not really. Others speak your praises –
my wife especially. Are you two lovers?
Are you just taking me for a ride,
ingratiating yourself before me in the mornings
after a wicked night between my sheets?

You don't help me much in that department.
Oh, I can get it up with you –
you're sexy enough and can taunt and tease
me into a frenzy. Oh, yeah, and you
keep me hard and I want to be with you.

You even make it easier for my wife
and I to fall into each others arms,
and we still make passionate love –
I won't let you insinuate yourself
between our sheets – not completely.

After being with you for a time though,
I just can't come when we're entwined.
Oh, she lets me take her from behind,
gives me head, jumps on my bones
and gyrates until our loins are afroth with foam

and I love being able to move my hips
in this frenzied dance as long as you let me.
It's great not to fire a salvo in pre-ignition
or have to storm the gates with a wet noodle.
You don't dampen my libido or enthusiasm.

But when I do hit the big O, it's not
like I hit any bell with a sledge:
it almost hurts and I don't get
the big crescendo or spontaneously say
Here we go! Before we fly off the cliff together.

It's a release and a relief to know
all systems are go when that particular
piston fires and thrusts me deep inside her
on the down stroke. And I can certainly
make her engine purr. And I do.

You have other quirks I'm not fond of too.
You make me clammy. My forehead is
always breaking out in a dew and I
have to mop you from my brow in ways
that make me look guilty of something –

or nervous when I'm in front of a class
or reading. I'm not nervous and I don't
like that. Sometimes you make me dizzy
and sweat profusely. It's not just the extra
baggage I'm carrying on a forty-four frame.

And as for my stools, you either
make me loose as a toothpaste tube
or issueth hard nuggets begrudgingly.
There doesn't seem to be any pleasing you.
You're a high maintenance bitch sometimes.

So how can you and I be friends?
My highs just aren't as high without
the lows. When we're together I don't get
so angry, true, and I am able to live
with your outbursts too. We're just not simpatico.

Do I get in the little fifty mg with you,
careen around every street with my
thinning hair streaming, a smile on my face?
Or do I banish you to the outer Hebrides
of my soul and hone my anger to a blade?

It's a tough call and tough duty
riding with you. I get scared. My
butt cheeks want to pull cotton
right out of the seat sometimes.
I don't know where you're taking me.

Little serotonin re-uptake inhibitor,
you keep my molecules humming
and I love the way you make my engine purr,
but I don't want my cylinders re-bored,
I don't want to be chopped and modified.

I'm a four-banger at heart. Dependable,
if not always reliable. And when I fly
off the proverbial handle looking for
a misplaced pen or correcting misplaced
modifiers, I at least own my emotions.

Others may want to disown me at times,
and I admit, without you, I am no one's
cup of tea or long cool drink of water.
I'm a little Napoleon who wants to pull
his bone apart. Always horny, frequently irate.

I'm a little volcano, a magma pool
of seething hates and grumbles. I erupt,
I spew, I froth and bubble and pop.
I leave a bad smell in a room after
I've erupted. My wife sometimes hates me.

So, my fine weather friend, what do we do?
Fuck each other senseless? Re-tool my genes
hot grooves? Re-gap my spark plugs?
Let you consume my dendrites in a brush fire
until I'm calm and have no fuel to burn?

You're an insidious little molecule
and I don't know whether you'll be
the death of me or I'll be the death of you.
Just don't get uppity with your glib talk
of designer genes, increased energy and joy, O.K.?

If we have this little chat now and again
and I talk of throwing you over for that
other daemon or muse, and anger turns
its blade to my own heart and mind,
you'll understand: we're not friends.

You may not be Mother's Little Helper.
You might not wheedle and cajole
to have your way with me. You might not
even be able to seduce me with your
velvet voice and sultry, sexy ways,

but you don't have to. I'll ride along
with you for a while – maybe longer.
I'll love my wife, make peace with
my other demons if need be. But
I'm not about to crown you queen for a day.

My muse doesn't run on high octane fuel.
She doesn't have high cheek bones
and 3500 p.s.i. pneumatic lips or
blade like hips. Her ass certainly can't
pull nails out of the wall,

but she makes my little fireman's hat
glow red, and when I enter the burning house
with her, the conflagration that consumes us
burns with an even glow and my synapses
crackle and send sparks aloft. Oh, they do!

So do me a favor, Zelda baby.
Don't get all up in my body the way you do.
Take a back seat once in a while. Don't grab
at my staff of life and blow the walls apart
when you blow me. Don't shake my fever tree.

Don't go down on me when I'm driving either.
I mean, I like it – I do – but it makes it
hard to control the car, and I like
who I'm becoming. I really do. That's not
a boast or idle braggadocio either.

Let Pinnochio's nose grow and sniff out
what it came here for. Roses certainly, the
particular piquancy of my real muse.
I've gotten used to her. I know her kinks.
We have a life time to iron out the wrinkles.

Boy in a Red Shirt on a Trampoline

The little boy on the trampoline
tries so earnestly to please:
up, down, higher and higher,
as if, in reaching the still point
between the ascent and the descent,
he could slow the rhythm of his heart's
own tympanic beat to the elastic
rhythm of his breathing, the soft
slow sproing of his stocking feet
against and in the very weave
of the exact center of the trampoline.

See how he brings his legs together,
how he point his toes just so,
legs slightly apart when he alights,
arms like bird wings in the bath,
shaking off the last drops of sunlight
from his splayed fingertips –
a phoenix of ambition arising
from the ash of his own gracelessness
to say "Look! Look at me!",
sweat flying like welding sparks
from his forehead and his hair.

But there are no spotters now;
his mother and father, who would
break his every fall and prevent him
from catapulting past the perimeter
of the springs and sky-blue frame
of this last perfect summer day,
are bouncing to a slacker weave
in a different city, a different season
half a continent away. And still,
the child in him jumps, jumps
up, down, higher and higher
while the sun leaks like orange pekoe
through the tight weave of the backyard fence.

He does a perfect forward somersault now,
arms clapped to his side, knees tucked up
and tight into his abdomen, chin to chest –
while over his right shoulder the foetal moon
rolls listlessly in its own amniotic heaven.
Up, down, higher and higher
he would jump for you,
now arching his back,
arms stretched out in a perfect
crucifix, feet inscribing the sky
in a backwards somersault –
head at six, feet at twelve –
his smile a perfect excision in time.

Right now he wishes his body could
align itself perfectly with yours,
to determine once and forever
the precise azimuth of desire.
He wants desperately and always
to land on his feet,
to please the man with
the salt and pepper beard,
looking out a back window,
steaming ceramic mug in hand,
about to taste the sunset at his lips.